ENIGMAS *of* HISTORY

THE MYSTERIES IN THE NAZCA DESERT

WORLD BOOK

a Scott Fetzer company
Chicago
www.worldbook.com

World Book edition of "Enigmas de la historia" by Editorial Sol 90.

Enigmas de la historia
La lineas de Nazca

This edition licensed from Editorial Sol 90 S.L.
Copyright 2013 Editorial Sol S.L. All rights reserved.

English-language revised edition copyright 2015
World Book, Inc.
Enigmas of History
The Mysteries in the Nazca Desert

WORLD BOOK and the GLOBE DEVICE are registered
trademarks or trademarks of World Book, Inc.

World Book, Inc.
233 North Michigan Avenue, Suite 2000
Chicago, Illinois 60601 U.S.A.

For information about other World Book publications,
visit our website at **www.worldbook.com** or call
1-800-967-5325.

Library of Congress Cataloging-in-Publication Data
Lineas de Nazca. English
 The mysteries in the Nazca Desert. -- English-language
revised edition.
    pages cm. -- (Enigmas of history)
  Includes index.
  Summary: "An exploration of questions surrounding
the geoglyphs (symbols marked in the earth) in the
Peruvian desert, known as the Nazca Lines. Features
include fact boxes, biographies of famous experts on
the Nazca Lines and the Nazca culture, places to see
and visit, a glossary, further readings, and index"--
Provided by publisher.
  ISBN 978-0-7166-2676-3
  1. Nazca Lines Site (Peru)--Juvenile literature. 2. Nazca
culture--Peru--Juvenile literature. I. World Book, Inc.
II. Title.
F3429.1.N3L52513 2015
985'.01--dc23
                           2015009349
Enigmas of History Set ISBN: 978-0-7166-2670-1

Printed in China by Shenzhen Donnelley
Printing Co., Ltd., Guangdong Province
1st printing May 2015

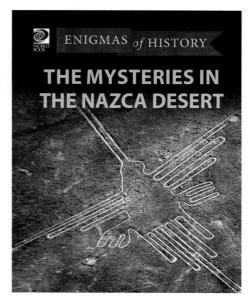

The Nazca lines are large designs, or geoglyphs,
etched in the earth; this geoglyph depicts a
hummingbird.

© Travelpix/Alamy Images

Staff

Contents

6 The Wonders in the Nazca Desert

10 The Lines in the Nazca Desert

18 The Nazca Desert

20 Types of Lines

22 Designs

24 Who Were the Nazca People?

28 A Giant Astronomical Calendar?

32 Archaeology from the Sky

34 Were the Lines Drawn from the Ground?

36 A Link Between the Lines and Art?

38 The Nazca Legacy

40 Was the Culture Lost to a Catastrophe?

42 Places to See and Visit

44 Glossary

45 For Further Information

46 Index

48 Acknowledgments

The Wonders in the Nazca Desert

Almost 2,000 years ago, an ancient culture cut hundreds of gigantic figures and lines into the barren desert plain in southern Peru. How and why did the Nazca people create these mysterious images that can only be seen from the sky?

Ever since they were first seen by airline pilots flying overhead in the 1920's, the Nazca lines have been regarded as a mystery. The enormous figures, called *geoglyphs*, etched into the Earth cover almost 400 square miles (1,000 square kilometers) of the flat desert floor between the Nazca and Ingenio rivers of southern Peru. Modern scientists have marveled that the Nazca people could have constructed such huge designs without being able to view them from the air. The images include line drawings larger than a football field depicting such animals as a condor, a hummingbird, an *orca* (killer whale), a fox, and a monkey. Other geoglyphs are of such geometrical figures as spirals, zig-zags and *trapezoids* (four-sided figures). In addition, more than 1,000 miles (1,600 kilometers) of straight lines are etched into the desert, passing over the rugged landscape with scarcely any curves or bends.

There are many unanswered questions about these lines. Do the Nazca lines represent animal gods, or were they messages intended to be viewed by the gods? Why did the Nazca people move thousands of tons of earth and rocks to make these designs in the desert that they could not see themselves? How did they make them? After all, many people believe that the Nazca people, who lived on the desert edge of the South American *pampa* (plain) more than 2,000 years ago, had little or no complex technology.

For nearly a century, *astronomers* (scientists who study the sun, moon, planets, and stars), engineers, artists, *anthropologists* (scientists who study humanity and human culture), historians, mathematicians, and ordinary people have proposed theories about the Nazca lines. Some of the more outlandish theories suggest the Nazca designs were made for *extraterrestrials* (beings from other planets) and that the straight lines were runways for their spaceships. Others believe that the Nazca lines are filled with special, secret powers. Scientists understand, however, that the key to decoding the Nazca lines must lie in the study of the people who made them thousands of years ago. So, any understanding must begin with a detailed examination of the lines and the *material remains* (objects left behind) of the Nazca *culture* (way of life).

Most scientists believe the massive geoglyphs had great religious significance to the Nazca people. Some experts believe the Nazca people walked along the lines as part of a religious ritual. Experts on the cultures of South America know that *processions* (parades) of people walking along complex lines cut into the earth are an important part of rituals among the people of the Andes Mountains. Some scholars believe that rituals of walking the Nazca lines were designed to urge the gods to bring water to the *pampas* (plains) by way of underground canals so the people could grow crops. Others believe the Nazca lines have an *astronomical* (sky) connection, perhaps serving as a giant calendar. Study of the lines continues. A Japanese archaeological team identified new figures in 2011 and 2012. But the many mysteries of the Nazca lines have yet to be completely solved.

NAZCA PLAIN
Dry river beds crisscross the
straight lines made by humans
in the Nazca Desert.

The Lines in the Nazca Desert

The Nazca lines were discovered over a century ago, and in the years since, researchers have asked the same questions over and over: What are the Nazca lines? How and when were they made? What was their purpose?

Although the first written source to mention lines in the desert around Nazca is an account from the 1500's by a Spanish *conquistador* (conqueror), the real discovery of the lines begins in 1926. In September of that year, three scientists were exploring near Ica on the southern coast of Peru. They were searching for traces of the long-lost Nazca people, a little-known yet fascinating culture that flourished between 300 B.C. and A.D. 800. German-born *archaeologist* (scientist who studies past cultures) Max Uhle (1856-1944) first described the Nazca culture in 1901, after he spent years searching South America to discover the source of beautiful painted pottery acquired by his museum in Berlin. The team in the 1920's was made up of Julio César Tello (1880-1947), considered the father of Peruvian archaeology; one of his students, Toribio Mejía Xesspe (1896-1983); and American *anthropologist* (scientist who studies human culture) Alfred L. Kroeber (1876-1960). One afternoon, when the sun was getting low in the sky, the two archaeologists climbed to the top of a small hill which overlooked much of the vast and empty expanse of sand and gravel that

is the Nazca desert. Highlighted by the low-angle light, they saw what appeared to be a series of amazingly straight lines or paths—or possibly ancient canals—that crisscrossed the landscape and vanished into the distance. Some of the lines seemed to outline certain areas and form drawings of strange figures. The Nazca lines were discovered.

Toribio Mejía Xesspe provided a fuller description of the Nazca lines to other scientists for the first time at the International Congress of Americanists meetings in Lima, Peru, in 1939. At this time he had developed a theory as to why they were built. He interpreted the lines as sacred paths, but he was not able to explain exactly how they were used. Mejía Xesspe was more concerned with the study of the ancient *aqueducts* (channels) and complex irrigation works that the Nazca culture had developed in the area over many centuries to allow them to raise crops in the dry land. The meaning of the strange Nazca lines remained in the background. In the 1940's, historian Paul Kosok (1896-1959) traveled to the *arid* (dry) desert territory on the coast of Peru after hearing about the work of Toribio Mejía Xesspe. On his trip, he did something that would

THE HUMMINGBIRD

This is one of the most well known Nazca figures because it combines geometric lines with beautiful stylization. The *geoglyph* (figure drawn on the surface of the earth) is almost 328 feet (100 meters) long, and it can only be seen completely from the air.

forever change the thinking about the Nazca lines: he boarded an airplane. Kosok flew over most every valley on the southern Peruvian coast from north to south. Within a large triangle-shaped region of flat desert, bounded by the towns of Nazca and Palpa, between the sea and the foothills of the mountains, Kosok saw long lines and well-defined triangular and *trapezoidal* (four-sided) etchings covering an area of about 300 square miles (776 square kilometers) that were perfectly visible from the air. He also spotted enormous figures drawn on the desert ground that represented *anthropomorphic* (human shaped) beings, animals, plants, and other unusual shapes. Kosok drew some of the designs he saw from the airplane on paper. They immediately reminded him of the motifs and designs he had seen in museums on paintings and pottery of the ancient Paracas and Nazca cultures of Peru. The figures were of gigantic proportions and were completely visible only from the air. From the ground, the figures disappeared and were impossible to see as a whole.

Kosok was not the first person to see the Nazca lines from the air. Aircraft pilots during the 1930's who worked the few commercial flights between Lima and cities to the south had already seen them. However, Kosok was the first to publicize them and study them closely. Kosok hiked the hills and plateaus around Nazca. He sketched the many circles, geometric shapes, spirals, and zigzags he saw in the desert and managed to capture the shape of many of these large *geoglyphs* (earth designs), including one that seems to show a bird in flight. Kosok deduced that the builders of the Nazca lines must have possessed at least a basic knowledge of mathematics.

ASTRONOMICAL EXPLANATION

Paul Kosok spent many years studying ancient *aqueduct* (channel) and irrigation systems in Peru. He realized that the Nazca lines were not channels used for moving water, since the lines etched into the desert surface were too shallow to serve this purpose. He thought that there may be a connection to *astronomy* (study of the sky), as he noticed that the lines seemed to have some connection with the movement of the sun and the stars. For example, Kosok observed that during the winter *solstice* (when the sun is at its greatest distance from the equator) on June 22 in the Southern Hemisphere, one of the Nazca lines seemed

MORTUARY ART

A skull with feather headdress (above). Along with weaving, feather ornaments were characteristic of the art of the Nazca culture. The most prized feathers came from birds in the Amazon region.

HUMAN FIGURES

One of the best-known *anthropomorphic* (humanlike) Nazca figures is the Owlman (above right), with his large eyes, round head, and hand pointing to the sky. While some people have suggested the figure represents an ancient astronaut, scholars agree the figure actually depicts a fisherman.

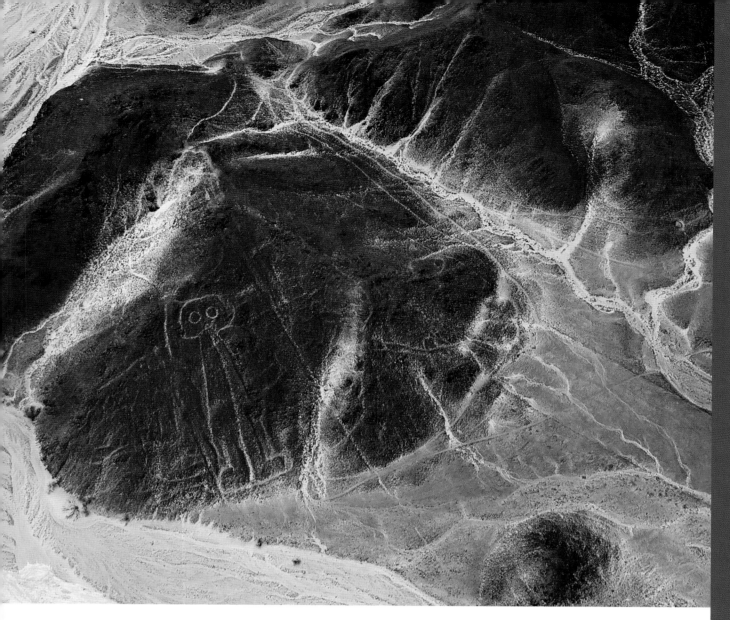

to point exactly toward the sun on the horizon.

Kosok communicated some of his ideas to a person who, over time, would become a legend among Nazca researchers, Maria Reiche (1903-1998), a German teacher who arrived in Cusco, Peru, in 1932 to work as a governess in the house of the German consul in the city and later in Lima. In Lima, she had the opportunity to do some work for the Museum of Archaeology. One day, she met Paul Kosok, who was looking for someone who could translate his articles into Spanish. This was the beginning of a partnership that would last for years. Kosok's descriptions of the Nazca

lines and the sketches and other work he showed to Reiche ignited her imagination. She first traveled to Nazca in December 1941. The desert region made such a profound impression on her that she would devote the rest her life to the study of the Nazca lines.

MAJOR DISCOVERIES
When World War II (1939-1945) broke out in Europe, Peru declared war on Germany in 1940. Aside from her one visit in 1941, Maria Reiche was unable to return to the pampas of Rio Grande near Nazca until 1946, after the war had ended. That year, she discovered and investigated the stylized drawing of a giant spider,

150 feet (46 meters) long, etched in the desert landscape. Kosok returned to the United States in 1949, where he continued his study of the Nazca culture. But by this time Reiche had settled in a small cabin, with no water or electricity, on the edge of the desert to always be near the Nazca lines. Day after day, facing the heat, dust, and vast solitude of the Nazca desert, she continued her research. She swept miles of sand with a broom to clean the etched grooves that formed the lines. People in the nearby town of Nazca made fun of her as "the woman who sweeps the desert."

Over the following decades, armed with a measuring tape, sextant, compass, and a ladder to view the Nazca lines from at least a few feet above, she made a detailed study of over 1,000 lines and designs etched in the desert floor. The Aerial Photographic Service of the Peruvian Air Force eventually provided her with aerial photographs of the Nazca area, which greatly assisted her study. She agreed with Kosok that the Nazca lines represented what she called "the largest astronomy book in the world."

The profits from her first book about the lines, *Mystery of the Desert* (1949), supported her research and efforts to protect the lines from destruction. In 1952 Reiche discovered the amazing figure of a monkey. She associated this design with the constellation *Ursa Major* (the Big Dipper), which would have announced the arrival of summer. She identified other figures that she associated with the passing of seasons, such as a Condor, Spider, and *Orca* (killer whale). With these, Reiche believed that the ancient Nazca had inscribed the most important *astronomical* (relating to the sky) events of their time in the earth of the *pampas* (plains).

Her first scholarly work, *The Giant Drawings on the Ground of the Nazca and Palpa Plains*, was published in English, German, and Spanish in 1969. This work featured a detailed description of the lines and an essay where she suggested that the lines and geoglyphs functioned as a calendar for the Nazca people. She also proposed her ideas about how the designs and lines were produced.

Other scholars had taken notice of the Nazca lines after Kosok and Reiche published their research. In 1949, German archaeologist Hans Horkheimer (1901-1965) published a paper in which he claimed that the lines "had a sociological sense" and defined the spaces as places reserved for dance and ancestor worship by people of the ancient Nazca culture. He argued that the lines may have served as a message to the gods, perhaps a request or an offering, in addition to their use in religious processions and dances. Horkheimer noted that while the Nazca lines are very artistic, many figures have surprisingly realistic features. For example, the giant figure of a South American monkey, one of the most famous of the Nazca designs, is quite realistic. However, he points out that there are some mistakes in the lines, either due to carelessness or for some other reason. For example, the tail of the monkey, which folds over the body in a huge coil, should actually curl downward as it normally does among South American monkeys.

Peruvian historian Fernando Silva Santisteban (1929-2006) proposed the idea that the figures in the Nazca lines represent the *mythical* (legendary) founding animals of the different *clans* (family groups) that existed in Nazca society.

IS WATER THE KEY?
Archaeologist Johan Reinhard (1943-) linked the Nazca lines with Andean religion, fertility gods, and the need to channel water in the harsh, arid environment of the region. He is among a growing list of scholars who believe that water is the key to solving the mystery of the enigmatic Nazca geoglyphs. Ancient springs ring the pampa around Nazca. These connect to a vast system of aqueducts, called *puquios* (POO key ohs), that demonstrate the importance of water to the Nazca people. In essence, Johnson argues that the lines serve as a giant map of valuable water sources in a dry land.

Anthony F. Aveni, professor of anthropology and astronomy at Colgate University in New York,

Anthony F. Aveni
(1938-)

American professor of astronomy and anthropology at Colgate University (New York State), Anthony F. Aveni is a world authority on the subject of prehistoric astronomy. He pioneered this field beginning with his in-depth study of pre-Columbian cultures in South America. From that perspective, he analyzed the Nazca lines for years and proposed interesting theories, including the possible relationship between the geoglyphs and ground water present throughout the pampas of Nazca.

PRACTICAL MAGIC
Aveni associated the direction of the lines with the sources of rivers and streams, without excluding the magical aspects of the lines.

Hans Horkheimer
(1901-1965)

Peruvian historian and archaeologist of German descent, he considered the lines to be sacred paths and drawings to serve as representations of the clans that made up the people who live in the Nazca Plain. Horkheimer also thoroughly studied other ancient cultures of Peru. Additionally, he delved into the issue of staple crops in pre-Columbian Peru and their crucial relationship with the political, religious, and social organization of its cultures.

FUNERARY WORSHIP
Horkheimer linked the Nazca figures with *funerary* (burial) worship and considered the region a ritual center.

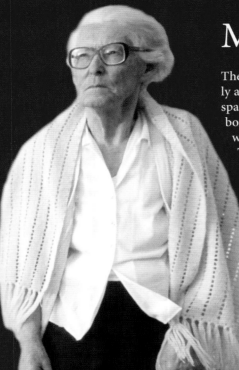

Maria Reiche **(1903-1998)**

The life of the researcher most closely associated with the Nazca lines spanned most of the 1900's. She was born in 1903 in Dresden, Germany, where she studied mathematics. This knowledge was of great use when she devoted herself to studying geoglyphs in Peru. In 1932, she traveled to Peru and remained there until her death. During her early years in Peru she worked as a teacher and nanny, but a fortunate encounter with archaeologist Paul Kosok led her to discover her true vocation: studying the Nazca lines. Along with Kosok, she was the main driving force behind the idea that the lines and figures were an example of ancient astronomy.

Perhaps even more than her academic work, Maria Reiche is also noted for her persistent and tireless efforts to preserve the lines from deterioration caused by nature and human development. In 1994, she witnessed the culmination of her efforts when UNESCO declared the Nazca lines a World Heritage Site.

PRESERVATION
In addition to carefully analyzing the Nazca geoglyphs, Maria Reiche took on the demanding task of protecting, restoring, and guarding the lines for many years, almost in total solitude.

"These highly intelligent people found a site that nature seems to have prepared as an immense canvas and where they made enormous drawings."

Paul Kosok

(1896-1959)

Although the Nazca lines had been discovered a dozen years earlier, it was American archaeologist Paul Kosok, of the University of Long Island, who rediscovered during the late 1930's the oversized figures drawn on the ground of the Nazca Plain. He was a pioneer in the systematic and scientific investigation of the lines and included young Maria Reiche in his work. He returned to his country in 1949 but continued to study the mystery of Nazca until his death a decade later.

PRECURSOR
Kosok advanced the idea of the connection between the large drawings of the Nazca Plain and the sun, stars, and constellations.

Cahuachi, Ceremonial Center

Located on the bank of the Nazca River, a few miles from the city of the same name and from its famous geoglyphs, Cahuachi (*CAH wah chee*) was the center around which the Nazca people led their lives. Built entirely of *adobe* (unfired clay), it occupies an area of 11 square miles (29 square kilometers) and has been described as "the largest adobe ceremonial center in the world." It consists of a number of buildings, including those known as the Great Temple and the Great Pyramid—the latter discovered in 2008—many of which are covered with soil due to the passage of time and have not yet been unearthed by archaeologists.

The Great Pyramid is 66 feet (20 meters) high and is made up of a series of terraces. Many of Cahuachi's structures are natural elevations that residents shaped according to their needs. Cahuachi was a pilgrimage site linked with the Nazca lines. It had houses and workshops, but it never became what we would call a city.

The site was occupied as long ago as the 300's B.C., before the establishment of the Nazca culture. With the Nazca culture, the site reached its peak between A.D. 100 and 400. After that time, it appears that Cahuachi was abandoned due to a series of floods that destroyed the place, although it remained a pilgrimage site for centuries until another flood came around the year 1000 ,which ended all activity at the site.

Another important building in Cahuachi is the Tiered Temple (below), the walls of which are decorated with the Chakana (the "Andean cross"), a symbol of the cosmos.

Hidden Treasures

Most of the structure of Cahuachi is still buried. Archaeologists such as Helaine Silverman and Giuseppe Orefici—who for decades have been researching and working on-site—made huge efforts to uncover the history of the place. Several fine *ceramics* (pottery) and crafts decorated with drawings characteristic of the Nazca culture were found on a natural slope. Examples of the fine *textiles* (fabrics) made by these people were also found, astonishingly well preserved.

DECORATIONS IN CAHUACHI

The Chakana, or "Andean cross," characteristic of pre-Columbian Andean towns, adorns several walls in Cahuachi.

SACRED CRAFTSMANSHIP

The *ceramics* (pottery) found in Cahuachi include vases, pieces with animal themes, and musical instruments.

PLACE OF THE SEERS
Panoramic view of the north face of the "Great Pyramid" of Cahuachi, one of the great sacred sites of ancient Peru. A possible meaning of its name is "place of the *seers*" (people who foretell the future).

believes, like others, that the Nazca lines had important religious and practical value for the people who built them. Aveni has argued that the straight lines and geomet-ric forms were made as religious pathways walked by Nazca pilgrims. Such practices are common among people of the Andes Mountains of South America. These processions were held to plead with the mountain gods associated with weather and water. The traditions and rituals connec-ted with the lines may have formed part—perhaps all—of Nazca religious practice. The traditions and rituals were taught by one generation to the next. Based on his computer analysis of the geometry of the Nazca lines, Aveni claims that the long, straight lines form a pattern of spokes that meet at specific locations where surface water enters rivers at the edge of the dry pampa, or at other spots between ancient stream beds.

THE LEGACY OF MARIA REICHE
Beginning in the 1960's and 1970's, Reiche observed an increasing number of tourists coming to the desert. Attracted by the mysterious geoglyphs, they began to inadvert-ently destroy some of the lines, obliterating them with footprints, the wheels of automobiles, and the im-pact of landing private planes. Reiche hired guards to prevent uncontrolled access to the area and, along with her sister Renate, built a watchtower next to the Pan American Highway so that curious tourists could observe some of the Nazca lines from the road. Maria Reiche died in 1998, at the age of 95, after having dedicated five decades of her life to the study of the Nazca lines. Her work is still conside-red groundbreaking today. In 1994, coinciding with the inauguration of a museum named after her to honor her efforts, UNESCO declared the Nazca lines a World Heritage Site, thus protecting a cultural legacy that is as vast as it is mysterious.

The Nazca Desert

About 280 miles (450 kilometers) south of Lima, the Nazca lines are located in the desert of the same name, in an area that covers around 310 square miles (802 square kilometers). There are hundreds of lines and geometric figures and over 70 representations of such figures as animals. Such patterns made on the surface of the earth are called *geoglyphs*.

Only fully appreciated from the air

It is amazing that these lines and symbols can be completely seen only from the air when flying over the desert.

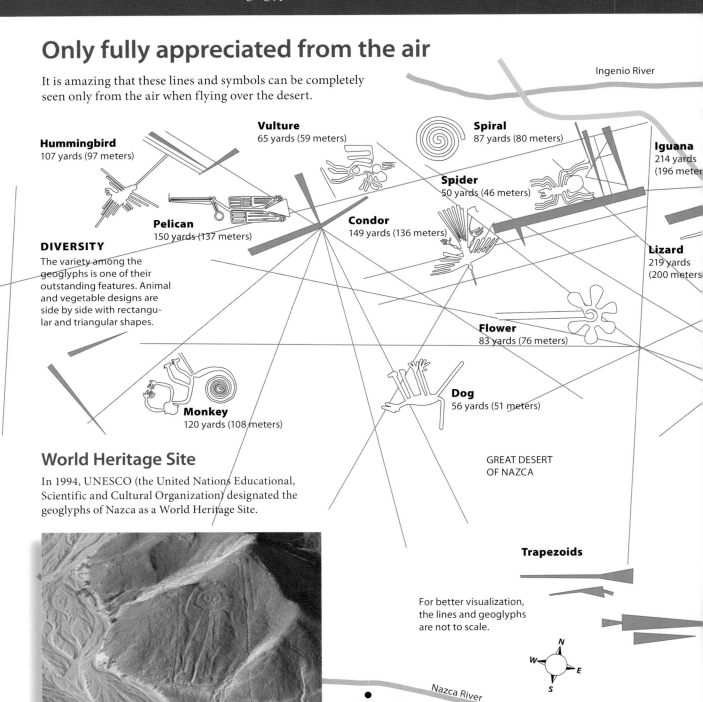

Ingenio River

Hummingbird
107 yards (97 meters)

Vulture
65 yards (59 meters)

Spiral
87 yards (80 meters)

Iguana
214 yards
(196 meter

Pelican
150 yards (137 meters)

Spider
50 yards (46 meters)

Condor
149 yards (136 meters)

DIVERSITY
The variety among the geoglyphs is one of their outstanding features. Animal and vegetable designs are side by side with rectangular and triangular shapes.

Lizard
219 yards
(200 meters

Flower
83 yards (76 meters)

Monkey
120 yards (108 meters)

Dog
56 yards (51 meters)

World Heritage Site

In 1994, UNESCO (the United Nations Educational, Scientific and Cultural Organization) designated the geoglyphs of Nazca as a World Heritage Site.

GREAT DESERT
OF NAZCA

Trapezoids

For better visualization, the lines and geoglyphs are not to scale.

N
W   E
S

Nazca River

●
Cahuachi

Why do the animals depicted in the geoglyphs belong to jungle environments?

The animals shown in many of the Nazca figures—such as the hummingbird, the spider, and the monkey—do not live in the desert climate of the Nazca region. Other animals represented, such as the orca (also sometimes called "shark"), are not land animals. Some scholars believe the representation of these animals is proof of a remote past when the climate of the Nazca region was humid and junglelike. It is more probable, however, that knowledge of wild animals on the coast of Peru came to the people who lived in the Nazca Desert via trade.

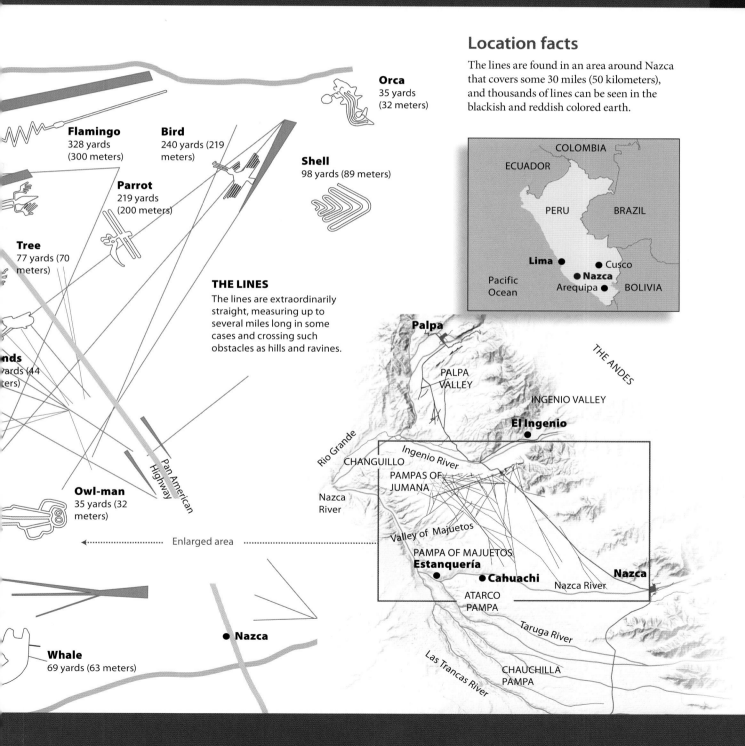

Orca
35 yards
(32 meters)

Flamingo
328 yards
(300 meters)

Bird 240 yards (219 meters)

Shell
98 yards (89 meters)

Parrot
219 yards
(200 meters)

Tree
77 yards (70 meters)

THE LINES
The lines are extraordinarily straight, measuring up to several miles long in some cases and crossing such obstacles as hills and ravines.

...nds
...yards (44 ...ers)

Owl-man
35 yards (32 meters)

Pan American Highway

Enlarged area

Whale
69 yards (63 meters)

● Nazca

Location facts

The lines are found in an area around Nazca that covers some 30 miles (50 kilometers), and thousands of lines can be seen in the blackish and reddish colored earth.

COLOMBIA

ECUADOR

PERU

BRAZIL

Lima ●
● Cusco
● **Nazca**
Arequipa
BOLIVIA

Pacific
Ocean

Palpa

THE ANDES

PALPA VALLEY

INGENIO VALLEY

El Ingenio ●

Rio Grande

CHANGUILLO

Ingenio River

PAMPAS OF JUMANA

Nazca River

Valley of Majuetos

PAMPA OF MAJUETOS

Estanquería ●
● **Cahuachi**
Nazca River
Nazca

ATARCO PAMPA

Taruga River

CHAUCHILLA PAMPA

Las Trancas River

Types of Lines

Most of the Nazca lines are long, straight lines or thin, trapezoidal outlines resembling arrows or airstrips. There are also figures shaped like people, animals, and flowers. Many of the lines were drawn on the level plain, but a few are found on the slopes of hills.

Types of Lines

Within the lines and symbols of Nazca, you can make out a variety of designs according to their shapes and possible meanings.

STRAIGHT, ZIGZAG, AND SPIRAL LINES

Lines can be found throughout the region of Nazca. Usually they measure about 3 feet (1 meter) wide and are about 1 mile (1.2 kilometers) long. Some are straight, others are in the shape of spirals or zigzags. They can be very precise or somewhat blurred, according to the period during which they were created.

STRAIGHT LINES

The hills and the uneven ground did not prove to be an obstacle for the Nazca people. Significant mistakes are not noticeable.

ZIGZAG LINES

The spacing between zigzags is very even.

GEOMETRIC SHAPES

There are thousands of lines and a variety of shapes all throughout the Nazca plateau region, in the valleys of Ingenio and Palpa.

TRAPEZOIDS

Four-sided figures with uneven sides, called *trapezoids*, are found throughout the Nazca plains. Elevated platforms are often found at the wide base of these figures.

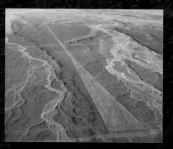

THE SPIDER

It is one of the best-known figures and is made of a single continuous line (like some labyrinths of medieval cathedrals). This reinforces the idea that the drawings were ritual paths.

ENTRANCE AND EXIT

Like other designs of Nazca, the spider has an entrance line and exit line, allowing you to travel the circuit without crossing lines.

TROPICAL ANIMAL

Characteristics of the Spider make it possible to identify it as a species of the Amazonian forest.

NATURAL FIGURES

Over 70 geoglyphs represent a variety of human, animal, and plant shapes. The direction of the lines maintains a geographic correlation. The theory most often put forth is that these symbols are an astronomical calendar.

THE HUMMINGBIRD

It is one of the most recently made geoglyphs and it has become a Peruvian icon. A set of extended parallel lines forms the bird's beak and is connected with other figures on the plateau.

Do the Nazca lines follow local ground-water channels?

For years a connection has been considered between the Nazca lines and the channels that the Nazca people built to tap ground water in the dry land. Researcher David Johnson suggested the idea that the markings and drawings pointed out underground-water channels rather than streams and other water sources on the surface. The proposal is intrig-uing, but there has not yet been sufficient evidence to support it.

Aerial vision

Researchers, such as Joe Nickell of the University of Kentucky, reproduced the Nazca figures using the technology that would have existed at the time, without aerial vision. With careful planning and simple techniques, a small group of people can recreate even the larger figures within a few days.

Nazca figures can be completely seen only from an airplane.

From an elevated tower, one can see the lines, but not clear figures.

On the ground, one can only see the dark rocks and the light ground.

SYMMETRY

The spider's jaws are drawn with a particular attention to matching the two sides that is not present in most of the Nazca drawings. A long straight line—made some time later—crosses through the drawing.

CELESTIAL MAP

Maria Reiche and her followers thought that the Spider is a representation of the constellation of Orion, although the little data that supports this idea is not conclusive.

THE GROUND

The surface is made up of a pebble layer of a dark reddish color, caused by oxidation, that covers another layer of light yellowish soil. Removing the surface stones produces the contrast in color.

Designs

Many of the extraordinary Nazca drawings have not been photographed very often, while others have gained extraordinary popularity, such as the Spider, the Monkey, and the Hummingbird. This is a small sample of some of the figures that are not so well known, although they are equally amazing and mysterious.

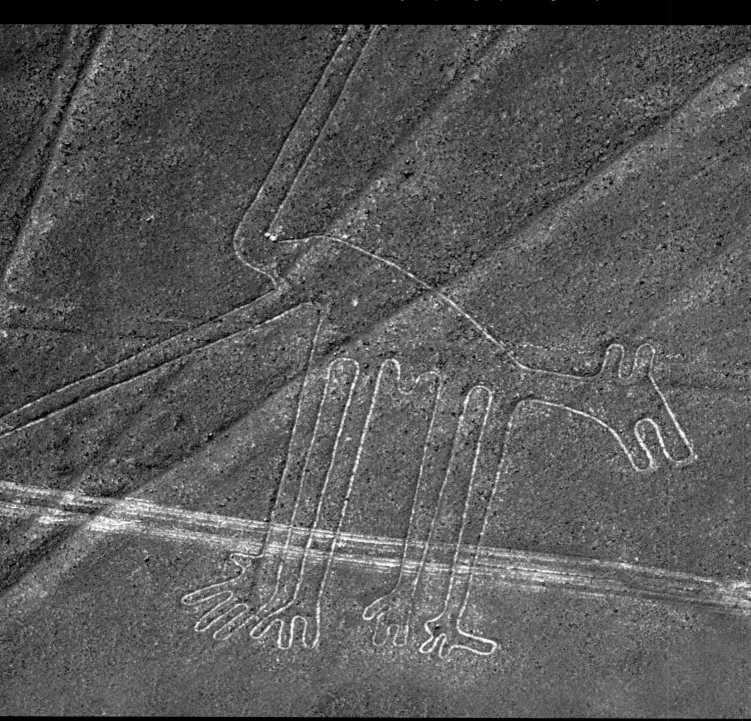

THE DOG

In the Way of Progress

The Pan American Highway crosses various Nazca geoglyphs without respecting these thousand-year-old designs. The road cuts through the middle of the Lizard figure, amongst others. When the road was built, the archaeological value of the lines was unknown. In the photograph at left, in addition to the Pan American Highway, you can see the observation tower built by Maria Reiche.

THE HANDS (above)   **THE ORCA** (below)

Who Were the Nazca People?

The Nazca lived in the dry valleys on the southern coast of Peru for over a thousand years. But they left few traces that allow scholars to understand their culture. Their beliefs and customs are largely still a great unknown.

The ancient Nazca people inhabited the valleys surrounded by the Chincha, Pisco, Ica, Rio Grande, and Acarí rivers in what is now southern Peru between about 300 B.C. and A.D. 800. *Archaeologists* (scientists who study past cultures) understand that the Nazca came from the older Paracas culture of that region. The few traces of Nazca culture that they left behind are known mainly from the tombs of their dead. The extreme dryness of the desert where the tombs are found has helped preserve many objects, especially pottery and textiles, that the Nazca buried with the dead. Nazca pottery includes beautiful *polychrome* (multicolored) bowls and other vessels and such musical instruments as pipes, drums, and rattles. The Nazca decorated much of the pottery with plant and animal designs. Some vessels are shaped like animals or people. The Nazca wove cotton and wool into colorful fabrics.

In the 1800's, many Nazca objects were stolen and sold by looters, and many objects were circulating in American and European museums and private collections. Archaeologist Max Uhle first studied Nazca *polychrome* (multicolored) pottery in Berlin in the 1880's, but at the time nobody knew exactly where such potter[y] came from. He went to South America a[nd] discovered the source of Nazca pottery i[n] southern Peru in 1901. However, scienti[fic] investigations of Nazca archaeological sites did not begin until 1952.

DID THEY LIVE IN CITIES?

Archaeologists have only found the ruin[s] of small villages in the Nazca region. Most archaeologists think the society w[as] relatively small. No Nazca cities have be[en] found, but the ruins of Cahuachi, locate[d] some 17 miles (27 kilometers) southwest [of] the modern city of Nazca, represents th[e] greatest population concentration of thi[s] culture. This walled complex was devel- oped around 300 B.C., and it has remain[s] of several buildings and a large open pla[za]. However, many scholars think this site was more likely a *ritual* (religious) cente[r] since no ruins of residential buildings h[ave] been found there.

Archaeologists believe Nazca society had a social organization based on *clans* (family groups), with villages ruled by chiefs. Villagers grew corn and other cro[ps] and raised *llamas*, a camel-like animal o[f] South America. In addition to their multicolored pottery, the Nazca people made simple musical wind instruments

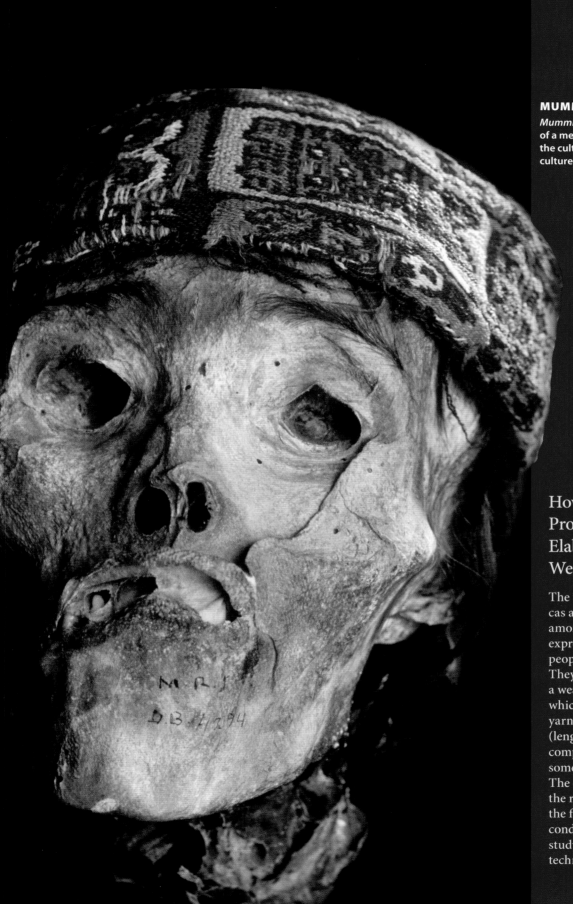

How Did They Produce Their Elaborate Weavings?

The textile art of the Paracas and Nazca cultures are among the highest artistic expressions of the native peoples of South America. They created designs with a weaving technique in which the *weft* (crosswise yarns) cross the *warp* (lengthwise yarns) in complex patterns using some 200 different colors. The extreme dryness of the region helped preserve the fabrics in near-perfect condition so experts can study and understand the techniques today.

Masters of Water

One of the most interesting things the Nazca culture left behind is the magnificent network of drains, aqueducts, channels, and subterranean *aquifers* (wells) they set up to supply water to their crops, showing the high level of agricultural development they reached. Over 40 filtering aqueducts have been found, as well as over 50 other channels. The water system is known collectively as *puquios*, which in Quechua (a local language) means "natural source."

Exquisitely decorated pitchers and pots have been found in some places inside the puquios, including a gold cup with a depiction of a water god in the form of an otter. The puquios system is unique to South America and some are still in use today. Scientists estimate that the large Nazca irrigation projects were carried out between 100 B.C. and A.D. 300, and that the puquios were built during the 400's.

and produced large quantities of wool fabrics. The Nazca wrapped their dead in many layers of woolen fabric and buried them in the desert seated in baskets and surrounded by offerings.

The Nazca culture declined between about A.D. 600 and 800. Scholars think that the Nazca culture eventually disappeared after the region was invaded by the nearby Tiwanaku and Huari peoples.

CONNECTED WORLDS

Although experts do not fully understand the Nazca religion, they think the Nazca shared many beliefs found among peoples of coastal Peru and the Andes Mountains. According to Peruvian historian Rebeca Carrión Cachot (1901-1960), the

religions of ancient Peru worshiped the forces and gods of fertility, and were inspired by the vital social need of supplying adequate food for the people through farming.

In Nazca culture, the principal gods reflected the dual nature of the environment surrounding them, as seen in the differences between day and night, the rainy season and dry season, and the sea and the land. In Nazca *myths* (stories), two forces of nature divided the world between themselves. They are represented by the *orca* (killer whale), which represented femininity and the capacity to cause death and to create life. A spotted cat, or jaguar, represents *agriculture* (farming) in the form of plants, corn, and trees. Both are frequently represented on Nazca pottery and

fabrics. They also appear as figures on a gigantic scale on the surface of the desert.

This dual worldview is common to many of the cultures of the Andes Mountains in South America. In addition to the many gods associated with the forces of nature, the Andean people believed in a *primordial* (original) creator of all things. Each community also had its own ancestor, which they worshiped and which united the families that made up a *clan* (family group). The people also worshiped their more recently deceased ancestors.

For the Nazca people, as in most Andean cultures, the worlds of the living and of the dead were closely interconnected. Sacred power was concentrated at burial sites and in

Sacred Skulls

"Trophy heads" are frequently found in Nazca art, demonstrating the ritual importance of head-hunting. The eyes and mouth of the head are sewn closed with cactus thorns, and there is a hole in the forehead. The severed head had a military significance connected to flaunting power over the enemy who was killed in battle or sacrificed. But it is also believed that the significance of the heads is connected to *shamanic* (priestly) practices related to fertility. The head also symbolizes supernatural powers and the regenerative seed of life.

PUQUIOS

Puquios were built of stone, in the shape of a spiral. Their shape helped add oxygen to the water and allowed access to the aqueducts for maintenance.

TROPHY HEADS

The cords that ran through the skulls of the trophy heads allowed the Nazca people to transport them or even hang them from a belt.

Music

The Nazca people produced ceramic musical instruments. This wind instrument is, like all the Nazca ceramics, brightly colored and decorated with symbolic designs.

such natural objects and locations as sacred stones, mountains, springs, caverns, and in religious idols.

Several myths of South America involve a goddess called Pachacámac, one of the most ancient religious figures in the region. Her name means "Queen of the World" in Quechua, an ancient language still spoken by many people in Peru today. In one myth, Pachacámac transforms a woman into a *vixen* (female fox) and a man into a monkey as a punishment. Among the Nazca lines, there is an enormous design of a dog (or vixen), and also of a large monkey. Many scholars think this demonstrates the Nazca religion shared many features with other, more well-known beliefs common among ancient cultures of South America.

A Gigantic Astronomical Calendar?

The creators of the Nazca lines had not developed writing, money, mathematics, or the wheel, and they did not produce iron. Nevertheless, between 300 B.C. and A.D. 700, they may have designed a giant astronomical calendar on the land.

Paul Kosok was the first person to connect the Nazca lines with the movement of the stars, but credit must be given to Maria Reiche for her careful analysis. Reiche developed the most widely accepted theory regarding the purpose of the Nazca lines. She thought that the lines were designed to determine the movements of certain stars and they would have functioned as a calendar. However, not all scholars agree with this interpretation.

In 1947, archaeologist Hans Horkheimer pointed out that many of the Nazca lines point north and south, where there are not any visible stars in the night sky. He also argued that such long lines were not necessary, and shorter lines could have easily been used to determine the exact position of a star in the sky, or where a star rises or sets. Horkheimer agreed with the idea that the Nazca lines and figures represent different *clans* (family groups) in Nazca society. In many cultures, clans are represented by a particular animal. He also believed that the lines were walked as sacred paths during religious celebrations or in the worship of ancestors.

Gerald S. Hawkins (1928-2003), an English astronomer, physicist, and mathematician, made the most serious argument against the theory, or idea, that the Nazca lines are a giant map of the stars. Hawkins had previously shown that Stonehenge in England had been an important astronomical calendar in ancient times. Using computer analysis, he checked the alignment of the Nazca lines against astronomical calculations on the positions of various stars from 5000 B.C. to A.D. 1900. In his book *A Secret of Ancient Peru* (1973), Hawkins found that some of the Nazca lines did point to the positions of the sun, moon, and particular stars over the past two thousand years, but it was no more than could be expected by mere chance.

BEYOND ASTRONOMY

Swiss art historian Henri Stierlin (1928-...) proposed a novel purpose for the Nazca lines. He based his theory on the Nazca people's great skill with weaving, as exemplified by a magnificent piece of seamless fabric found in Paracas in 1925 and the linens with which the Nazca people wrapped their dead. He argued in his book *Nazca:*

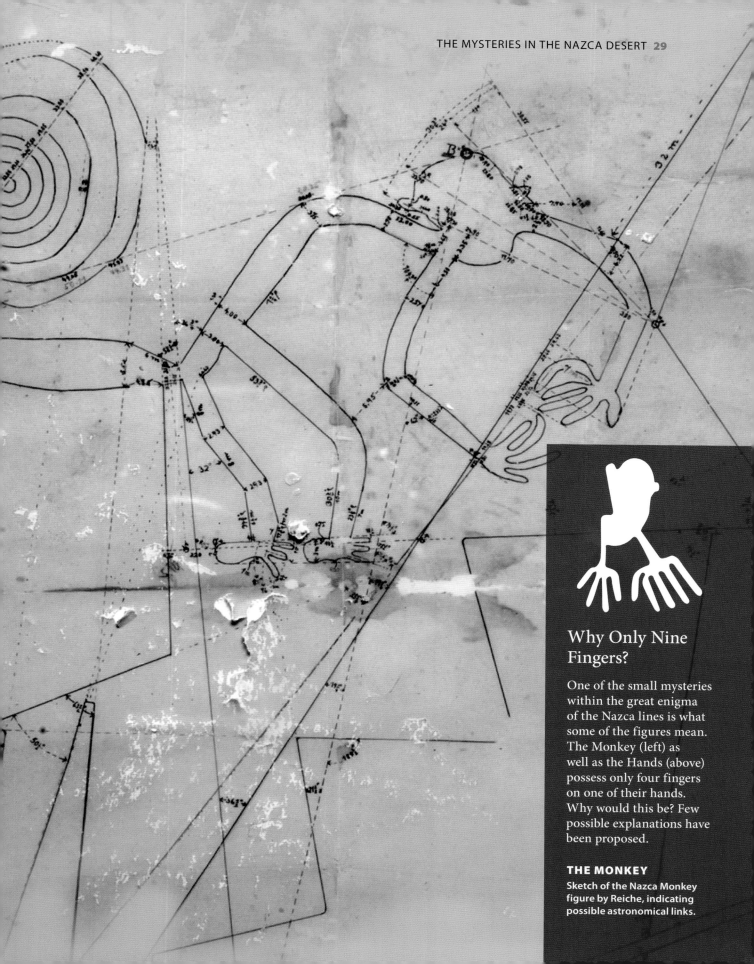

Why Only Nine Fingers?

One of the small mysteries within the great enigma of the Nazca lines is what some of the figures mean. The Monkey (left) as well as the Hands (above) possess only four fingers on one of their hands. Why would this be? Few possible explanations have been proposed.

THE MONKEY
Sketch of the Nazca Monkey figure by Reiche, indicating possible astronomical links.

The Key to a Mystery: Deciphering an Archaeological Enigma (1983), that instead of looking at "the largest astronomy book in the world," we are observing "the greatest open-air workshop for weaving ever created by man." He concluded that the Nazca dedicated a great portion of their time to weav-ing, so it is only natural that this dedication would be reflected in the lines, which he argued also had *ritual* (religious) significance.

American *archaeologist* (scientist who studies past cultures) and Andean expert Johan Reinhard observed that many of the Nazca lines converge on hills and mountains in the region. He does connect the Nazca lines to religion, but specifically related to water and fertility. According to his book, *The Nazca Lines: a New Perspective on Their Origin and Meaning* (1987), the lines point towards mountains that generate rain, an essential source of life for the Nazca in the *arid pampa* (dry plain). The Nazca people believed the mountains were the home of the gods.

Finally, Peruvian historian Fernando Silva Santisteban supports the theory that the Nazca lines and *geoglyphs* (earth designs) formed the basis of a system of social interaction among the people, and that certain images were associated with and served to identify the different clans that made up Nazca society. In this theory, he does not rule out the idea that the Nazca lines also had some astronomical function as a calendar. But he argues that such a function would have been very different from the modern concept of an astronomical observatory. "The Nazca calendar, if that is was it was," he stated, "would have been a record of phenomena, but not in the Western mathematical sense."

Water Canals

Another scholar who defends the ritual function of the lines but also associates them with water resources is Anthony F. Aveni of Colgate University in New York. According to Professor Aveni, the lines were built as paths for pilgrimages or rituals, and they would have been connected with the flow of ground water. In his book *Between the Lines* (2000), Aveni noted that many of the straight lines follow the direction of small river beds or irrigation channels. He verified that water would have been present at all of 62 points he mapped where lines meet (below). According to Aveni, the straight lines converge in spoke patterns and trapezoids where sources of surface water (irregular circles) enter the river valleys next to the pampa, or at certain points on elevated land between the ancient streambeds.

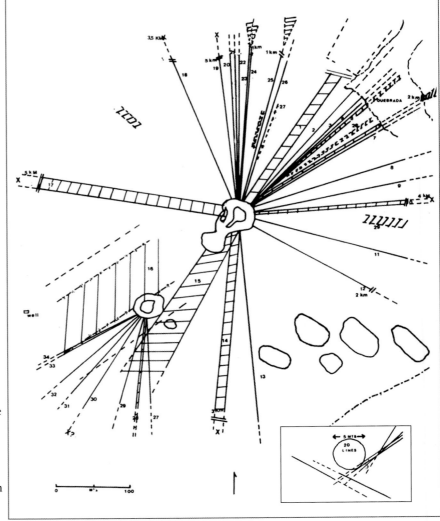

Magical Flights

Maria Reiche noted the likely religious importance of the Nazca lines and related them to the Andean god Kón, represented by the figure of a flying cat. Within the Nazca culture it was believed that this god appeared plowing the skies at a particular time of the year. But *anthropologists* (scientists who study human culture) Marlene Dobkin de Rios and Mercedes Cárdenas argue that the Nazca figures were related to the practices of *shamans* (medicine men) and their ritual use of sacred plants, especially the San Pedro cactus (*Trichocereus pachanoi*). When consumed, the cactus can change the way the person consuming it feels and experiences his surroundings. During drug-induced trances, Nazca shamans were said to "fly" and had the capacity to "see from above" as they connected with their spirit guide. This novel perspective suggests that the Nazca lines had a function that would also have been extended to curing disease, an important function of Nazca shamans. The image of the hummingbird, one of the most frequently represented creatures, reinforces this idea. In the Andes, this bird has a strong symbolic association with curing ceremonies of shamans. The idea of a flying cat that can look down from the heights like a bird was a common theme in the worldview of other Andean peoples. Thus, there is a relationship between the Nazca images and the fact that they can be best appreciated from the sky above.

LOOK BUT DON'T TOUCH

Walking on the Nazca lines, as scholars believe the Nazca once did, is forbidden, because foot traffic would damage the delicate geoglyphs. In the photo above, however, children are walking upon a geoglyph they made themselves. Teachers and students from the Maria Reiche School in Nazca drew a spiral in the desert using simple wooden poles, rope, and strong applied geometry concepts. The group then began a procession to cut the design into the earth.

Archaeology from the Sky

Images taken from above (whether from space satellites or from aircraft) have become invaluable tools for archaeology. Thanks to these images, structures have been discovered that were hidden due to vegetation, erosion, or the passage of time.

The Discovery of Cahuachi

Strangely, at times it is easier to see from the sky what is under the land. In October 2008, an Italian team of researchers discovered a pyramid, a ceremonial center of the Nazca culture, buried near the desert of Cahuachi (right, in a multispectral image), near to where other similar formations had already been found. They discovered the pyramid using multispectral images (including red and infrared wavelengths). The photographs were obtained by the Quickbird satellite and are a testimony to how far recent technology has gone in archaeological research.

HIDDEN STRUCTURES

The black arrows indicate structures made by humans that still need to be studied in depth.

VEGETATION

In the infrared images, vegetation appears as blue. The ground shows up as yellow.

ANCIENT RIVER

The red arrows indicate an ancient channel of the Nazca river: a sedimentary structure where there was once a water course.

Photograph Types

Various types of equipment are used to carry out surface investigations via aircraft. Regardless of the technology used, two types of images are usually taken for different purposes: oblique photographs, which give a greater perspective and a better representation of relief and topography in general; and vertical photographs, which are better for creating maps.

Oblique photograph

Vertical photograph

Recognition from the Air

The discovery of a pyramid buried near Cahuachi (right, in an ordinary photograph) by means of satellite observation reminds us—almost 80 years later—of the moment in 1939 when Paul Kosok viewed the drawings made of the Nazca Plain from the air. Since the first hot-air balloons were in use (at the end of the 1700's), and the invention of photography (some decades later), aerial archaeology has been an important tool in the discovery and study of the remains of past civilizations.

PYRAMID
This ridge forms part of the outline and corners (white arrows) of a pyramid shape that can barely be distinguished under the ground.

What Is the Quickbird?

Launched into space in October 2001, Quickbird was a commercial satellite equipped with high-definition cameras.

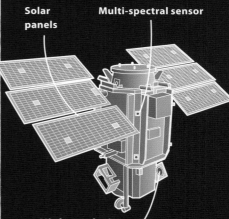

Solar panels

Multi-spectral sensor

High resolution camera

Crop Marks

Aerial photography allows the discovery of structures that are covered by vegetation and are not visible at first sight, as is shown in the drawing on the right. Buried foundations or walls limit the forest growth, while the buried ditches favor its development. These variations are known as crop marks.

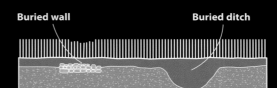

Buried wall

Buried ditch

Were the Lines Drawn from the Ground?

Evidence indicates that the Nazca lines were constructed in a simple and ingenious way from the ground. Much careful coordination was needed to ensure precise results, since the enormous images cannot be seen from the surface.

Modern observers have marveled that the Nazca could construct such huge designs without being able to view them from the air. Many experts have thought about this problem.

TOUGH TASK

Scientists know the Nazca lines were created by painstakingly removing millions of dark stones that cover the desert to expose the lighter subsoil, producing a channel about 12 inches (30 centimeters) deep. The rocks covering the *pampa* (plain) contain iron oxide, which forms a dark *patina* (coating) after centuries of exposure to sunlight and weather. This is in contrast to the yellowish underlying soil that has a high content of *gypsum*, a light-colored mineral. The ancient Nazca deposited the surface stones on both sides of the furrows in such a way that they formed small ridges. The designs have lasted for centuries in the desert environment, with little rain or wind to wear them away.

When Maria Reiche arrived in 1946, Nazca residents told her that a series of wooden posts once stood at regular intervals along the lines. Reiche concluded that the builders may have worked with small scale models and transferred the designs onto the desert floor section by section, marking each section with wooden posts. She believed the Nazca used a unit of measurement based on the proportions of the human body. But, *archaeologists* (scientists who study past cultures) have not found any evidence relating to such a method among the Nazca remains.

Peruvian archaeologist Roger Ravines Sánchez (1942-...)theorized that small, natural rises in the desert would have provided suitable vantage points for supervising the Nazca designs. Fernando Silva Santisteban has found that some of the drawings were made on the hillsides, so that the entire figures are visible in high-*relief* (shadow) when the sun is low.

Modern researchers have demonstrated that the Nazca designs can be constructed easily from the ground. The builders likely produced straight lines by sighting wooden poles along the desired path. They made spirals and curves guided by a rope attached to a fixed stake, producing an arc in much the same way one does on a piece of paper with a compass. Still, the huge figures and surprising straightness and accuracy of the Nazca lines continue to inspire a feeling of awe and mystery.

How Did They Withstand Wind and Rain?

It seems miraculous that the Nazca lines have withstood bad weather. Nevertheless, there is an explanation for the astonishing lack of change in the lines. The first factor to consider is the climate of the region. The rainfall is very low, and even though the Nazca plain is windy, the strong gusts of air moving over the plain do not find many obstacles, so most of the sand is drawn northward, where it is deposited in large dunes. In addition, the dark color of the soil and the high temperatures form a hot air cushion that reduces the wind speed a few inches above the ground, which then protects the surface from erosion. The dark color of the surface of the rocks is called "desert varnish," and it is a thin mineral layer that has been deposited on the rocks over the course of centuries. It is the removal of these rocks around the lines that allows the figures to stand out more. In addition, another very important variable must be taken into account: the gypsum in the soil around Nazca, when in contact with mild humidity, forms a mortar, or cement, that attaches the rocks to the ground, which has prevented the destruction of the ridges alongside each line.

How Were They Drawn?

The most widespread theory is the one that Maria Reiche, creator of the sketches reproduced below, always maintained. According to Reiche, the drawing would have been made in sections, using a measuring unit to transfer it to the ground.

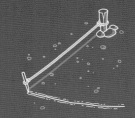

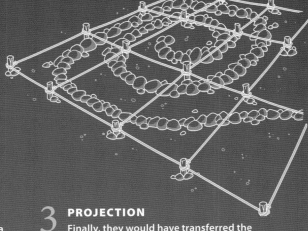

1 SCALE
They must have first prepared a small-scale drawing that would serve as a model which they could divide into sections.

2 MEASUREMENT
Then they must have used a measuring unit that would have worked by stretching out a rope in radial segments.

3 PROJECTION
Finally, they would have transferred the design to its actual size by first drawing the sections on the ground at their final scale and then reproducing the lines of the drawing, section by section.

EXPERIMENT

In 1984, British archaeologist Clive Ruggles recreated some Nazca lines using technology that would have been available at the time they were made.

A Link Between the Lines and Art?

There is a clear link between the images seen in Nazca folk art and the gigantic designs they made in the desert. The images depicted in the folk art are related to the religious beliefs of the Nazca people.

Finely made Nazca pottery reveals they were a sophisticated artistic culture. The *polychrome* (multicolored) pottery is generally adorned with geometric designs and complex *anthropomorphic* (humanlike) and *zoomorphic* (animal) representations. Nazca artists usually outlined figures in black, then filled them in with creamy white, orange, red, purple, and gray, but never green or blue. The colors were made with a mineral-based paint that was applied before the pottery was baked. Many vessels have characteristic "bridge handles," which join two spouts on the top.

The ancient roots of the Nazca artistic traditions are found among the Paracas culture that thrived from about 1200 B.C. to around 100 B.C. in the Ica region, not far from Nazca in southern Peru. Archaeologists do not know much about the Paracas, but they do know they were farmers who were experts at building *aqueduct* (channel) systems to move precious water to their fields.

AGE OF SPLENDOR

From the record of beautiful pottery and fabrics, it appears that Nazca culture flourished between about A.D. 400 and 600. Archaeologists believe most of the lines and *geoglyphs* (earth designs) were also made around this time. Many figures that appear on Nazca pots, jugs, bowls, vessels, and dishes are abstract representations of plants and animals. Many of these same designs appear in the Nazca geoglyphs. On pottery, there are also curious figures that have a mix of characteristics from different animals. These hybrid figures are often depicted with appendages in the form of worms, serpents, or plant stems. Sometimes these beings have two heads or contain another being inside their bodies. Sometimes their clothing is adorned with human heads.

Scholars do not fully understand the meaning of the different symbols seen in Nazca folk art. The Nazca had no writing, so our understanding of their beliefs comes from studies of other ethnic groups in the Andes region of South America who practiced their traditional religions when they were first contacted by European colonists. Many of the symbols that were important to these people are similar or identical to Nazca symbols. Scholars therefore believe they had much the same meaning.

Bird of Good Omen

Of the 30 large designs that the Nazca drew on the desert floor in the valleys between the Ingenio and Nazca rivers, 18 represent birds, creatures that the pre-Incan peoples identified with gods, as well as the sky and the day. They include condors and pelicans, and also hummingbirds, one of which (in the photograph) measures almost 320 feet (98 meters) long, with a wingspan of over 215 feet (66 meters). Those who support the theory of the astronomical function of the drawings often note that its large beak coincides with magnetic north. The hummingbird (native to the Americas, with some 100 species found in Peru) was often depicted by Nazca artists, both on fabrics and on pottery, and normally associated with elements such as flowers or cultivated seeds. Its symbolism was sacred, related to the concept of fertility and the practices of *shamans* (medicine men). Its representation was thought to favor an abundant harvest.

KNITTED BIRDS
Birds and flowers are interspersed in an edging on a Nazca cotton and wool weaving that dates to some time after 300 B.C.

The flower

Flowers also appear frequently in Nazca art. One of the Nazca figures depicts a flower with a stem formed from two long parallel lines that appear to have been added later. It is thought that, in reality, it could have been an image of the sun, particularly as it is seen during an eclipse, when the sun spots have an appearance similar to flower petals. Both ideas—which are not mutually exclusive—involve symbolism of the creation of life.

The Nazca Legacy

The Nazca culture goes far beyond its mysterious lines. It had excellent weavers, and its pottery is among the most refined in all of pre-Columbian South America.

Polychrome Pottery

The Nazca people inherited an extraordinary and inventive ability to work with textiles and pottery from their Paracas ancestors. While Paracas artisans were very good weavers, the Nazca are best known for their pottery. The Nazca are also considered the best painters in the Andean world. When their art was at the peak of its splendor, up to a dozen different color tones were being used on a single vessel. The animal themes (wild or supernatural) and the images of flowers and fruit were completed with astonishing detail and artistic perfection. Many of the designs on the pottery are repeated in the Nazca lines. This sculpture (right) is a figure of a musician playing a pan flute, or *siku*.

TWO-HEADED SERPENT

"Bridge handle" vessels (right) are characteristic of the Nazca culture. They have two spouts with a ceramic bridge in between. The two-headed serpent is a sacred symbol of the underworld, common throughout the Andes.

METALWORK

One of the less well known expressions of the Nazca culture is its metal handicrafts. The Nazca made detailed ornaments worked in fine sheets of gold. The most frequently made objects include pendants, breastplates, and masks. These pieces of art had a ritual value related to the sun, as the giver of life, while they also indicated social status, since their use was restricted to the higher social classes. The metalwork (left) is a gold funeral mask, with hair in the form of serpents. The extensions at the top of the mask end in figures of birds.

30.49.1

The Trophy Heads in Art

Some of the most notable cultural expressions from the Nazca world are the "Trophy Heads." Experts believed that the heads were obtained in battle against neighboring peoples, but more recent studies suggest that some of them actually belonged to the local population. The image on the left is a trophy head adorned with feathers.

Textiles

As worthy heirs to the Paracas culture—which had the best weavers in South America prior to the Spanish Conquest—the Nazca people knew how to make the highest quality yarns. They used llama and alpaca wool mixed with cotton and even human hair for their fabrics. The design themes found in their pottery are also captured in clothing and other fabrics. Fortunately, the dry climate of the Nazca desert helped preserve a large number of these textiles, something that was not possible for other cultures. The image below shows a groups of musicians and dancers made of yarn.

TRADITIONAL MUSIC

Music was an important part of the Nazca culture. This siku (above), a typical Andean wind instrument, is made of *terra cotta* (baked clay) wrapped with cording tied to a seashell.

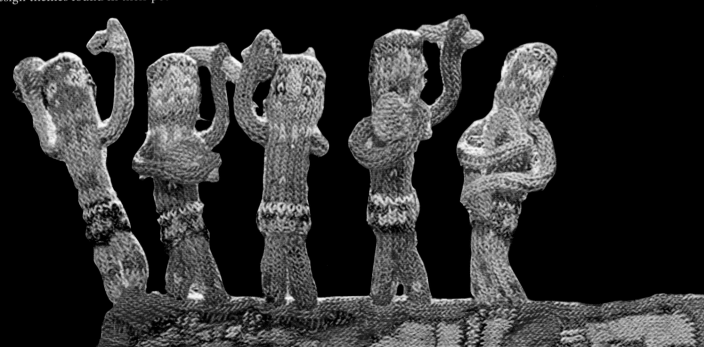

Was the Culture Lost to a Catastrophe?

Starting around A.D. 600, a series of crises began that would bring about the end of the Nazca culture.

Scientists know that the decline of the Nazca culture began around A.D. 600, mainly from the work of German *geologist* (scientist who studies the Earth) Georg Petersen Gaulke (1898-1985), who published his book *Evolution and Extinction of the Advanced Paracas-Cahuachi Cultures* in 1980. Among the possible causes that may have brought on the end of the culture, Gaulke lists overpopulation, a decline of available water, and the unstoppable advance of the surrounding desert. The desert eventually closed in on the once-fertile valleys that were home to the Nazca people for centuries, making the region uninhabitable.

In the *arid* (dry) environment of the Nazca region, even a minor decrease in the amount of water available could tip the delicate balance that existed between natural resources and the ability to sustain them over time. In 1958, Spanish *geographer* (scientist who studies a place or region) Gonzalo de Reparaz concluded that a prolonged *drought* (a long period without rain) occurred in the region. The drought increased the rate of water evaporation, leading to *salinization* (accumulation of salt) of the soil that made growing crops difficult. By about A.D. 800, signs of increasing social unrest, population decrease, cultural decline, warfare, and invasions by outside groups can be seen in the archaeological remains in the Nazca region. Soon after, the Nazca culture disappeared completely.

WEATHER EVENT

Overpopulation, overuse of water resources, and weather continue to cause problems today in southern Peru. Scientists today know of a phenomenon, called El Niño, that periodically occurs in the Pacific Ocean around Christmas and causes dramatic changes in weather. When El Niño occurs, changes in the ocean currents off northern Peru often result in heavy rainfall in southern Peru.

Scientists think that a series of exceptionally strong El Niño events affected the Nazca region between A.D. 500 and 600, causing severe floods, landslides, and serious damage to the *aqueduct* (channel) system they had built to irrigate their crops. The damage may have been too much to repair. This may have been what tipped the balance of nature against the Nazca culture, leading to its decline and eventual disappearance.

Excessive Exploitation

In a report issued at the end of 2009, a team from the McDonald Institute for Archaeological Research, at the University of Cambridge (United Kingdom), headed by David Beresford-Jones, suggested that the changes associated with the El Niño current would have been much less devastating if the Nazca population had not cleared extensive forests of trees called *huarango* for farmland. In addition to excellent wood, this hardy tree provided the Nazca with bark that could be pounded into cloth, resin for dye, flowers to attract bees, and seeds to feed livestock. It is probable that the people knew of the invigorating effect of the syrup made from its fruit, which is used today to make desserts and sweets in Peru. However, evidence suggests they were never aware of the fundamental role this tree played in maintaining the ecosystem. Today scientists know that the huarango tree has a remarkable capacity to increase soil fertility and moisture. The tree helps temper the dry conditions of the region, and its deep root system prevents erosion as it holds the soil when floods occur. The Nazca culture overharvested this valuable tree almost to extinction, which would have made the advance of the surrounding desert more rapid.

DESERTIFICATION
Remains of an irrigation canal from the Nazca culture. With the passage of time, erosion has left the canal above the level of the soil.

Places to See and Visit

PLACES OF INTEREST

MUSEO MARIA REICHE
NAZCA, PERU

The Casa Museo Maria Reiche, where Maria Reiche spent her last years as the main researcher of the Nazca lines, is located 17 miles (27 kilometers) from the city of Nazca. It has a collection of personal tools and materials that she used in her research. She is buried in the garden on-site.

CANDELABRO DE PARACAS
PARACAS, PERU

Paracas is a port city about 180 miles (287 kilometers) from Lima and is also the name of the culture that preceded the Nazca. The Paracas Candelabra, made using techniques similar to those used to make the Nazca lines, can be seen on the coast.

MUSEUMS OF ICA
ICA, PERU

The city of Ica is located about 91 miles (146 kilometers) from Nazca and has several museums. The Museo Regional de Ica has a collection of mummies and objects from the Paracas and Nazca cultures and a replica of the Nazca lines. The Museo Científico Javier Cabrera is where controversial stones, supposedly of *extraterrestrial* (alien) origin, are exhibited.

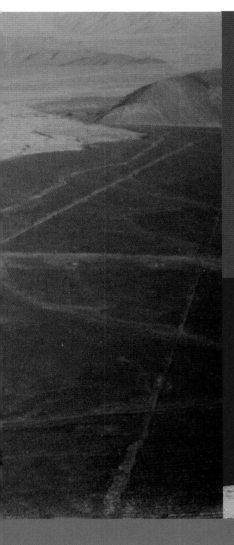

Nazca Pampa

THE CITY OF NAZCA

The capital of the Peruvian province of the same name is located some 280 miles (450 kilometers) southeast of Lima. The geoglyphs are located nearby. The Museo Antonini, dedicated entirely to the Nazca culture and the discoveries made by Italian archaeologist Giuseppe Orefici at the archaeological site of Cahuachi, is found in the city. You can also visit the Museo Municipal de Nazca.

ACCESS AND FLIGHTS

Tourists generally first arrive in Lima by airplane. From there you can take a domestic flight to Ica 164 miles (264 kilometers), or take a bus or car on the Pan American highway. From Ica, you can make a day trip to the geoglyphs, although the city of Nazca 91 miles (146 kilometers) from Ica also has a number of hotels. Light aircraft fly out of Nazca, although you can also schedule flights from Ica.

OTHER ATTRACTIONS

In addition to historical and archaeological treasures, the region includes places of natural beauty, such as the Paracas National Preserve, an extensive coastal area that takes its name from the town of Paracas, 47 miles (75 kilometers) north of Ica. The preserve was created to protect the maritime and coastal flora and fauna, especially the birds of the region. The Paracas resort has beautiful beaches for vacationers.

Cahuachi

The ceremonial center of the Nazca culture is located 17 miles (27 kilometers) south of the city of Nazca. Italian archaeologist Giuseppe Orefici has worked for nearly 30 years on what he considers "the largest adobe ceremonial center in the world." It is made up of several pyramids, in which valuable pottery shards have been found.

PALPA LINES
PALPA, PERU

In the same region as the Nazca lines is the Palpa Valley, a plain with geoglyphs similar to those in Nazca, although the age of these lines has not been determined. Some scientists believe the Palpa lines may be older than those of the Nazca.

NATIONAL MUSEUM OF ARCHAEOLOGY, ANTHROPOLOGY AND HISTORY OF PERU
LIMA, PERU

The oldest state museum of Peru and the largest in the country, the Museo Nacional de Arqueologíca, Anthropología e Historia del Perú has extensive permanent exhibits dedicated to the Pre-Columbian cultures of ancient Peru. It includes objects from the Nazca people and has a room dedicated to the Paracas culture.

PHOEBE A. HEARST MUSEUM OF ANTHROPOLOGY
BERKELEY, CALIFORNIA

Over 9,500 ancient Peruvian objects, gathered by Max Uhle, the German archaeologist who first identified the place of origin of Nazca style of pottery, are housed here. A great part of this collection comes from excavations of many intact tomb groups Uhle conducted between 1899 and 1905. Smaller but significant collections were contributed by professors John Rowe and Alfred Kroeber.

Glossary

Agriculture— The raising of crops and farm animals.

Anthropology— The scientific study of humanity and of human culture.

Anthropomorphic— Having a human form.

Aqueduct— An artificial channel for bringing water from a distance.

Archaeology— The scientific study of the remains of past human cultures.

Arid— Having little rainfall; dry.

Astronomy— The science of the sun, moon, planets, stars, and all other celestial bodies. It deals with their composition, motions, relative positions, distances, and sizes, as well as with Earth in its relation to them.

Clan— A group of related families that claim to be descended from a common ancestor.

Drought— A long period of weather without rain.

Extraterrestrial— Alien. Outside or originating away from Earth.

Fault— A break in the earth's crust, with the mass of rock on one side of the break pushed up, down, or sideways.

Geoglyph— Design or symbol marked into the ground.

Geography— The study of Earth's surface, climate, continents, countries, peoples, industries, and products.

Geology— The science that deals with Earth, its features, the layers of which it is composed, and their history.

Gypsum— A common, light-colored mineral.

Icon— An image, picture, or symbol.

Llama— A South American mammal, somewhat like a camel, but smaller and without a hump.

Mummified— A state of having been been preserved through natural or artificial means.

Myth— A story of unknown origin, often one that attempts to account for events in nature or historical events from long ago.

Orca— A killer whale.

Pampas— The vast, treeless, grassy plains of South America.

Patina— A film that develops on the surface of metal or rock, formed by contact with oxygen.

Polychrome— Having many or various colors.

Pre-Columbian— Of or belonging to the period before the arrival of Columbus in the Americas.

Quechua— The language of the Quechua people. Certain dialects of Quechua are still spoken in parts of Peru, Ecuador, and Bolivia.

Relief— Figures or designs that project from a surface in sculpture or carving.

Rituals— Religious ceremonies.

Salinization— The accumulation of salt, especially in the soil. It is often caused by a high rate of evaporation.

Shaman— A medicine man or person believed to possess magic powers, as over diseases or evil spirits.

Solstice— Either of the two times in the year when the sun is at its greatest distance from the celestial equator. In the Northern Hemisphere, the summer solstice, about June 21, is the longest day of the year, and the winter solstice, about December 21 or 22, is the shortest. In the Southern Hemisphere, the solstices are reversed.

Vixen— A female fox.

Trapezoid— A four-sided plane figure having two sides parallel and two sides not parallel.

For Further Information

Books

Fullman, Joe. *Ancient Civilizations*. New York: DK Pub.,
    2013. Print.

Hawkins, John. *The World's Strangest Unexplained Mysteries*.
    New York: PowerKids, 2012. Print.

Samuels, Charlie. *Technology in the Ancient Americas*. New
    York: Gareth Stevens, 2014. Print.

Silverman, Helaine, and Proulx, Donald A. *The Nasca*.
    Malden: Wiley-Blackwell, 2002. Print.

Websites

Geiling, Natasha. "Stunning Black-and-White Photos of the
    Nazca Lines." *Smithsonian.com*. Smithsonian, 23 Dec.
    2014. Web. 25 Feb. 2015.

"Lines and Geoglyphs of Nasca and Pampas De Jumana."
    UNESCO World Heritage Centre. UNESCO, 2015. Web.
    25 Feb. 2015.

"Nasca Lines: Decoded." *National Geographic Channel*.
    National Geographic, 2013. Web. 25 Feb. 2015.

"Nasca Lines: The Sacred Landscape." *National Geographic*.
    National Geographic, 2015. Web. 25 Feb. 2015.

Index

A

Adobe, 16, 43
Agriculture, 7, 26, 33, 40, 41. See also Water
Andean cross, 16
Andes Mountains, 7, 17, 26
Anthropologists, 7, 31
Aqueducts, 10, 12, 14, 26, 36, 40
Aquifers, 26
Archaeologists, 10-17, 32-33
Art, 36-39. See also Pottery; Textiles
Astronomy, 7, 12, 14, 28-30
Aveni, Anthony F., 14-17, 30

B

Beresford-Jones, David, 41
Bird figures, 19, 37. See also Condor (figure); Hummingbird (figure)
Burials, 14, 26-28

C

Cahuachi, 16, 24; aerial view, 32-33; map, 18-19; visiting, 43
Calendar. See Astronomy
Canals, 7, 10, 30
Candelabra (figure), 12-13, 42
Cané, Ralph, 14
Cárdenas, Mercedes, 31
Carrión Cachot, Rebeca, 26
Ceramics. See Pottery
Clans, 14, 24, 26, 28, 30
Condor (figure), 14, 18

D

Desert varnish, 35
Dobkin de Rios, Marlene, 31
Dog (figure), 18, 22, 27
Drought, 40

E

El Niño, 40, 41
Extraterrestrials, 7, 42

F

Fertility, 14, 26, 30, 37
Flowers, 18, 37

G

Gaulke, Georg Petersen, 40
Geoglyphs, 6-7. See also Nazca lines
Great Pyramid, 16-17
Great Temple, 16
Gypsum, 34, 35

H

Hands (figure), 18-19, 23, 29
Hawkins, Gerald S., 28
Horkheimer, Hans, 14, 28
Huarango trees, 41
Hummingbird (figure), 10-11, 18, 20, 31, 37

I

Ica (Peru), 10, 42
Iguana (figure), 18-19
International Congress of Americanists, 10
Irrigation. See Water

J

Jaguar (figure), 26
Johnson, David, 14

K

Kón, 31
Kosok, Paul, 10-15, 28
Kroeber, Alfred, 10, 43

L

Lima (Peru), 10, 12, 13, 19
Lizard (figure), 18-19, 23

M

McDonald Institute for Archaeological Research, 41
Medicine, 31
Mejía Xesspe, Toribio, 10
Metalwork, 38
Monkey (figure), 14, 18, 27, 28-29
Mummies, 25, 42
Museo Antonini, 43
Museo Maria Reiche, 42
Music, 24, 27, 39
Mystery of the Desert (Reiche), 14
Myths, 26, 27

N

National Museum of Archaeology, Anthropology, and History of Peru, 43
Nazca (Peru), 24, 42, 43
Nazca culture, 6-7, 24-27; decline and disappearance, 26, 40-41; early research, 10; religion, 24, 26-27; social organization, 24-26
Nazca Desert, 6-9; advance of, 40-41; map, 18-19
Nazca lines, 6-7; aerial views, 6, 12, 13, 18-19, 21, 32-33; animal representations, 19, 28; as astronomical map, 7, 12, 14, 28-30; discovery, 10; folk art and, 28-30, 36-37; Kosoc's research, 10-13; map, 18-19; method of drawing, 34-35; missing fingers, 29; preservation efforts, 15, 17, 31; recreating, 21, 34, 35; religious importance, 7, 14, 17, 31; types of, 20-21; visiting, 42-43; water resources and, 14-17, 30; weather resistance, 35
Nickell, Joe, 21

O

Orca (figure), 14, 19, 23, 26
Orefici, Giuseppe, 16, 43
Overpopulation, 40
Owl-man (figure), 9

P

Pachacámac, 27
Palpa lines, 43
Pampas, 6, 7, 34, 43
Pan-American Highway, 17, 23
Paracas (city), 28, 42, 43
Paracas culture, 24, 25, 28, 36, 38-39,
   42
Paracas National Preserve, 43
Parrot (figure), 9
Pelican (figure), 18
Peru, 6, 13; places to visit, 42-43
**Phoebe A. Hearst Museum of
   Anthropology,** 43
Polychrome pottery, 24, 36, 38
Pottery, 10, 16, 24, 38, 43; bridge
   handles, 36, 38; figures on, 26, 36;
   Nazca lines and, 36, 37
Puquios, 14, 26-27
Pyramids, 16-17, 32, 33

Q

Quechua, 27
Quickbird satellite, 32-33

R

Ravines Sánchez, Roger, 34
Reiche, Maria, 17, 31, 42; discoveries,
   13-15; on drawing of lines, 34, 35;
   on lines as calendar, 14, 21, 28, 29
Reinhard, Johan, 14, 30
Religion, 17, 24; art and, 36, 37;
   importance to lines, 7, 14, 17, 31;
   in Nazca culture, 26-27
Reparaz, Gonzalo de, 40
Rowe, John, 43
Ruggles, Clive, 35

S

Salinization, 40
San Pedro cactus, 31
Serpent, 38
Shamans, 31, 37
Shell (figure), 9
Silva Santisteban, Fernando, 14, 30
Silverman, Helaine, 16
Skulls, 12, 27
Solstices, 12
Spider (figure), 13, 14, 18, 20-21
Spiral (figure), 18
Stierlin, Henri, 28-30
Stonehenge, 28
Sun, 12-13, 28, 37, 38

T

Tello, Julio César, 10, 42
Textiles, 16, 24, 25, 38, 39; figures on,
   26; meaning of lines and, 28-30,
   36-37
Tiered Temple, 16
Tombs, 24, 43
Trapezoids, 6, 12, 18-20, 30
Tree (figure), 9
Trophy heads, 27, 39

U

Uhle, Max, 10, 24, 43
UNESCO, 7, 17
Ursa Major, 14

V

Vulture (figure), 18

W

Water: disappearance of Nazca culture
   and, 40-41; importance to lines,
   7, 12, 14-17, 30; network for
   supplying, 26-27, 36
Weaving. See Textiles
Whale (figure), 9
Writing, 28, 36

Acknowledgments

Pictures:

© ACI

© Age Fotostock

© Corbis Images/Cordon Press

© Cordon Press

© Getty Images

© iStockphoto